SIGHT WORDS

3rd Grade Workbook

(Baby Professor Learning Books)

SPEEDY PUBLISHING

Speedy Publishing LLC
40 E. Main St. #1156
Newark, DE 19711
www.speedypublishing.com

AGAINST

in opposition to (someone or something)

against

against

Use it in a sentence.

BLOCK

a solid piece of material (such as rock or wood) that has flat sides and is usually square or rectangular in shape

block

block

Use it in a sentence.

CHANCE

an opportunity to do something;
an amount of time or a situation in
which something can be done

chance

chance

Use it in a sentence.

CATTLE

cows, bulls, or steers that are kept on
a farm or ranch for meat or milk

cattle

cattle

Use it in a sentence.

CHEW

to use your teeth to cut food into small
pieces before you swallow it

chew

chew

Use it in a sentence.

DIRECTION

the course or path on which
something is moving or pointing

direction

direction

Use it in a sentence.

EXCITE

to cause feelings of enthusiasm in
(someone); to make (someone) feel
energetic and eager to do something

excite

excite

Use it in a sentence.

HUNT

to search for something or someone
very carefully and thoroughly

hunt

hunt

Use it in a sentence.

INSTEAD

as a substitute or equivalent

instead

instead

Use it in a sentence.

MASTER

a person holding an academic degree higher than a bachelor's but lower than a doctor's

master

master

Use it in a sentence.

PACKAGE

a box or large envelope that is sent
or delivered usually through the mail
or by another delivery service

package

package

Use it in a sentence.

QUITE

to a very noticeable degree or extent

quite

quite

Use it in a sentence.

REMAIN

to be left when the other parts are
gone or have been used

remain

remain

Use it in a sentence.

SPEND

to use (money) to pay for something

spend

spend

Use it in a sentence.

STREAM

a natural flow of water that is smaller than a river

stream

stream

Use it in a sentence.

SPEAK

to say words in order to express your thoughts, feelings, opinions, etc., to someone

speak

speak

Use it in a sentence.

SPREAD

to open, arrange, or place
(something) over a large area

spread

spread

Use it in a sentence.

STRETCH

to make (something) wider or longer by pulling it

stretch

stretch

Use it in a sentence.

SPECIAL

different from what is normal or usual

special

special

Use it in a sentence.

SUDDENLY

happening, coming, or done very quickly
in a way that is usually not expected

suddenly

suddenly

Use it in a sentence.

SUPPOSE

to think of (something) as happening or being
true in order to imagine what might happen

suppose

suppose

Use it in a sentence.

TEAM

a group of people who compete in a sport, game, etc., against another group

team

team

Use it in a sentence.

TRAVEL

to go on a trip or journey; to go to a place
and especially one that is far away

travel

travel

Use it in a sentence.

UNITED

involving people or groups working
together to achieve something

united

united

Use it in a sentence.

WIRE

a thin, flexible thread of metal

wire

wire

Use it in a sentence.

WORSE

less pleasant, attractive, appealing,
effective, useful, etc.

worse

worse

Use it in a sentence.

WHETHER

which one of the two

whether

whether

Use it in a sentence.

WARN

to tell (someone) about possible danger or trouble

warn

warn

Use it in a sentence.

YOURSELF

your normal or healthy self

yourself

yourself

Use it in a sentence.

Visit

BABY PROFESSOR
EDUCATION KIDS

www.BabyProfessorBooks.com

to download Free Baby Professor eBooks
and view our catalog of new and exciting
Children's Books

CPSIA information can be obtained
at www.ICGtesting.com
Printed in the USA
BVHW010319251021
619810BV00023B/510